COMING TO GRIPS WITH
HELL

ERWIN W. LUTZER

MOODY PRESS
CHICAGO

Coming to Grips with
HELL

" **H**ell disappeared. And no one noticed."

With that terse observation American church historian Martin Marty summarized our attitude toward a vanishing doctrine that received careful attention in previous generations. If you are a churchgoer, ask yourself when you last heard an entire sermon or Sunday school lesson on the topic.

A recent *Newsweek* article says, "Today, hell is theology's H-word, a subject too trite for serious scholarship." Gordon Kaufman of Harvard Divinity School believes we have gone through a transformation of ideas, and he says, "I don't think there can be any future for heaven and hell."

Admittedly, hell is an unpleasant topic. Unbelievers disbelieve in it; most Christians ignore it. Even the staunchly biblical diehards are often silent out of embarrassment. Hell, more than any doctrine of the Bible, seems to be out of step with our times.

REASONS TO DISBELIEVE

There are, of course, reasons this doctrine suffers obvious neglect. At the top of the list is the difficulty of reconciling hell with the love of God. That millions of people will be in conscious torment forever is beyond the grasp of the human mind. Bishop Robinson, who gained notoriety with his liberal views in *Honest to God*, writes,

> Christ . . . remains on the Cross as long as one sinner remains in hell. That is not speculation; it is a statement grounded in the very necessity of God's nature. In a universe of love there can be no heaven that tolerates a chamber of horrors; no hell for any which does not at the same time make it hell for God. He cannot endure that, for that would be a final mockery of his nature. And He will not.[1]

The doctrine of hell has driven many people away from Christianity. James Mill expressed what many have felt. "I will call no being good, who is not what I mean by good when I use that word of my fellow creatures; and if there be a Being who can send me to hell for not so calling him, to hell I will go."[2]

One man said that he would not want to be in heaven with a God who sends people to hell. His preference was to be in hell so that he could live in defiance of such a God. "If such a God exists," he complained, "He is the devil."

To put it simply, to us the punishment of hell does not fit the crime. Yes, all men do some evil and a few do great evils, but nothing that anyone has ever done can justify eternal torment. And to think that millions of good people will be in hell simply because they have not heard of Christ (as Christianity affirms) strains credulity. It's like capital punishment for a traffic violation.

Second, serious thinking about hell all but disappeared because of the medieval distortions that have become associated with this place of torment. Dante in *The Inferno* describes his tour through hell with vivid images of demons who tear sinners apart with claws and grappling hooks if they can catch them before they sink beneath the boiling pitch. He depicted the judgment of God in exact symbolic retribution. If a person used music in this world in the service of evil, demons will blow trumpets into his ears so that fire gushes out of his ears, eyes, and nostrils.

Such medieval authors took biblical teaching and combined it with pagan mythology resulting in caricatures that are still with us. We should note in passing that the Bible teaches that Satan and his demons will be the tormented, not the tormentors. The suffering of hell (to be discussed later) will be meted out by God, not inflicted by one sinful being onto another.

A third reason belief in hell has waned is because of the growing acceptance of reincarnation. Twenty-four percent of Americans now profess to believe that they will reappear in a different body. Shirley Mac-Laine says it is like show business. "You just keep going around until you get it right."

If liberalism allows us to believe in God without an afterlife, reincarnation enables us to believe in an afterlife without God. Thus millions of Westerners believe in some kind of afterlife, but it is one of bliss, not misery. Genuine fear of suffering in hell has vanished from the mainstream of Western thought. Few, if any, give prolonged thought to the prospect that some people will be in hell. Fewer yet believe they them-

selves will be among that unfortu-
nate number.

THE ECLIPSE OF HELL

For liberal Protestants, hell be-
gan to fade in the nineteenth century.
The universalists believed God was
too good to send anyone to hell, and
the Unitarians concluded that man
was too good to go there. United
Church of Christ theologian Max
Stackhouse said, "The prevailing
opinion is that when you die you're
dead but God still cares." Rabbi Ter-
ry Bard, director of pastoral services
at Boston's Beth Israel hospital, sums
up the view of many Jews: "Dead is
dead," he says, "and what lives on
are the children and the legacy of good
works."

And what about evangelicals
who believe in the complete trust-
worthiness of the Bible? University
of Virginia sociologist James Hunter,
who has written two books on con-
temporary evangelicalism, says,
"Many evangelicals have a difficult
time conceiving of people, especially
virtuous nonbelievers, going to hell."
He makes the point that according to
evangelical theology, Ghandi should
be in hell; but Hunter says that when
evangelical students were asked
about that, they became "extremely
nervous." To say that good people

who are not born again will be in hell is so difficult to accept that many evangelicals are now saying, "I think there is a hell, but I hope it will be soul-sleep."

At a symposium at Trinity Evangelical Divinity School in Deerfield, Illinois, in May 1989, a heated discussion arose as to whether those who disbelieved in eternal punishment could properly be called evangelicals. Though the denial of eternal hell is found among liberals and groups such as the Jehovah's Witnesses and Seventh Day Adventists, it has never been taught within mainstream Christianity. Yet, it is now seeping into evangelicalism, too. Though there was no denunciation of such views in the final draft of the conference (Evangelical Affirmatives '89), we must ask the question anew in this generation: Does the Bible teach that unbelievers will live forever in conscious torment or not?

ALTERNATE TEACHINGS

There are two alternate views that vie for acceptance in response to that question. The first is called universalism, claiming that in the end all will be saved. The other seeks to show that the Scriptures teach conditional immortality, that is, only the righteous live forever, whereas unbelievers are judged and then annihilated. They are thrown into the fire that consumes them.

All sensitive people cringe at the thought of multitudes in perpetual misery. No one wants to think that God would consign human beings to such punishment. If either of these views can be defended from the Bible we would most gladly accept such interpretation of the data. Let's consider these alternatives with an open mind, testing them by the only standard that matters, the Word of God.

UNIVERSALISM

Universalism teaches that since Christ died for all people without exception, it follows that all will eventually be saved. God will overcome every remnant of evil, and all rational creatures (some would even include Satan) will eventually be redeemed.

One of the earliest and most influential defenders of universalism was Origen, a scholar from North Africa (A.D. 185-254). He defended Christianity and expounded the Scriptures but was also the father of Arianism (the denial of Christ's deity) and of the belief that all would eventually be saved. He taught that even Satan would be reconciled to God.

Origen's teaching was condemned at the Council of Constantinople in 543 and was not taught in the church until several hundred years later when John Scotus Erigena (A.D. 810-877) embraced essentially the same teaching. He argued that since God was one, His will was one, and therefore all men were predestinated to salvation.

Scriptural support for universalism is found in passages that picture the final state as one of total subservience to God. Paul taught that in the fullness of time, there would be the "summing up of all things in Christ, things in the heavens and things upon the earth" (Ephesians 1:10). And it is God's intention to "reconcile all things to Himself, having made peace through the blood of His cross; through Him, I say, whether things on earth or things in heaven" (Colossians 1:20). The implication, we are told, is that everyone will eventually be brought into the family of God.

Unfortunately this attractive interpretation has serious weaknesses. If the universalist's interpretation were correct then Satan would also have to be redeemed, that is, reconciled to God. Yet it is clear that Christ did not die for him (Hebrews 2:16); therefore God would have no just grounds to pardon him, even if he repented.

What is more, the Scriptures explicitly teach that he along with the beast and the false prophet shall be "tormented day and night forever and ever" (Revelation 20:10). Here we have a clear statement that Satan shall never be redeemed but will exist in conscious eternal torment.

Yes, everything will be summed up in Christ, but that means that all things will be brought under Christ's direct authority. Christ has completed everything necessary to fulfill God's plan of salvation. The order of nature shall be restored, and justice will prevail throughout the whole universe. As we shall see later, that restoration does not negate the doctrine of hell but instead necessitates it.

Other passages are used to teach the eventual salvation of all men. Paul wrote, "So then as through one transgression there resulted condemnation to all men, even so through one act of righteousness there resulted justification of life to all men" (Romans 5:18). A similar passage is 1 Corinthians 15:22: "As in Adam all die, so also in Christ all shall be made alive." Universalists interpret these verses to mean that as all men are condemned for Adam's offense, so all men are justified by Christ's act of righteousness.

Unfortunately, that interpretation fails for two reasons: first, the texts must be interpreted in light of others that clearly teach the eternal misery of unbelievers in hell. We simply do not have the luxury of isolating passages of Scripture.

Second, we must realize that the Bible frequently uses the word *all* in a restricted sense, as pertaining to all in a certain category rather than all without exception. Examples are numerous. Matthew tells us that "all Judea" went out to hear John the Baptist (3:5-6). Luke records that a decree went out that "a census be taken of all the inhabited earth" (2:1). And the disciples of John the Baptist complained that "all men" were following Christ. In the passages written by Paul, it is clear that all who are in Adam die, whereas all who are in Christ shall be made alive. The *all* has limitations built into it by the context.

The final death blow to universalism is in Matthew 12:32. Christ is speaking of the unpardonable sin: "It shall not be forgiven him, either in this age, or in the age to come." In Mark 3:29 it is called an "eternal sin," indicating that it begins in this age and is carried on for all eternity without hope of reversal. How could those

14

who have committed this sin be reconciled to God when Scripture clearly says they shall never be forgiven?

The New Testament is so filled with warnings to those who do not turn to God in this life that universalism has never been widely accepted by those who take the Bible seriously. Obviously if this teaching were true, there would be no pressing reason to fulfill the Great Commission or to urge unbelievers to accept Christ in this life.

CONDITIONAL IMMORTALITY

Whereas universalism sought to take the "forever" out of hell, we now come to a theory that attempts to take the "hell" out of forever. Conditional immortality is more attractive to evangelicals than universalism. This teaching contends that all will not be saved, but neither will any be in conscious torment forever. God resurrects the wicked to judge them, then they are thrown into the fire and consumed. The righteous are granted eternal life while the unbelievers are granted eternal death. Hell is annihilation.

Clark Pinnock of McMaster University in Toronto, Canada, asks how one can imagine for a moment that the God who gave His Son to die on the cross would "install a torture chamber somewhere in the new creation in order to subject those who reject him in everlasting pain?'' He observes that it is difficult enough to defend Christianity in light of the problem of evil and suffering without having to explain hell too.

Pinnock believes that the fire of God consumes the lost. Thus God does not raise the wicked to torture them but rather to declare judgment on them and condemn them to extinction, which is the second death. Everlasting punishment, according to Pinnock, means that God sentences the lost to final, definitive death.

Perhaps the most scholarly defense of this doctrine was written by Edward Fudge in his book *The Fire That Consumes*. In it Fudge claims that only God has unqualified immortality. He had no beginning and has no end. As for souls, they have all been created and can be destroyed. Only the righteous are granted eternal life. The idea of the indestructibility of the soul comes from Plato, we are told, not from the New Testament. This belief was accepted by Christians, and thus it was natural to draw the conclusion that the souls of unbelievers are tormented forever. This popular medieval teaching was adopted by the Reformers and thus is associated with orthodoxy.

Obviously it is not possible to reproduce all of Dr. Fudge's arguments here. But in summary, his view turns on the interpretation of several phrases that are used in the Bible to refer to the end of the wicked. Specifically, Fudge says that whenever the word *eternal* is linked to words of action, it refers to the result of the action, not to the action itself. For example, the phrase "eternal judgment" does not mean that the judgment itself will go on eternally, though there will be consequences that will. "Eternal redemption" does not mean the the act of Christ goes on forever, though the consequences do.[3]

Now Fudge applies that theory to such passages as 2 Thessalonians 1:9 where Paul writes that when Christ comes He will deal out retribution to the wicked who will "pay the penalty of eternal destruction, away from the presence of the Lord and from the glory of His power" (2 Thessalonians 1:9). The question is whether the phrase *eternal destruction* means conscious torment or annihilation. According to Fudge, eternal destruction is annihilation and will take place when Christ returns. It is eternal in the sense that the consequences (extinction) will go on forever. The phrase "eternal punishment" and the word *perish* are interpreted in the same way. The fire of hell consumes its victims and obliterates them.

Unfortunately, that interpretation will not survive careful analysis. Robert A. Morey in his book *Death and the Afterlife* points out that the word *destroyed* as used in the Bible does not mean "to annihilate." The Greek word *apollumi* is used in passages such as Matthew 9:17; Luke 15:4; and John 6:12, 17. In none of those instances does it mean "to pass out of existence." Morey writes, "There isn't a single instance in the New Testament where *apollumi* means annihilation in the strict sense of the word."[4] Thayer's *Greek-English Lexicon* defines it as "to be delivered up to eternal misery."

Let's consider another text. Christ says that the lost will go into "eternal fire," which has been prepared for the devil and his angels. And then He adds, "And these will go away into eternal punishment, but the righteous into eternal life" (Matthew 25:46). Since the same word *eternal* describes both the destiny of the righteous and the wicked, it seems clear that Christ did not mean that their punishment would be swift and short. Eternal punishment implies that the wicked will experience it eternally. We must ask: In what sense would punishment be eternal if the wicked were annihilated? Clearly Christ taught that both groups will exist forever, albeit in different places. The same eternal fire that Satan and his hosts experience will be the lot of unbelievers.

The eternal conscious existence of unbelievers was already taught in the Old Testament. Daniel wrote, "And many of those who sleep in the dust of the ground will awake, these to everlasting life, but the others to disgrace and everlasting contempt" (12:2). The wicked will experience shame and contempt for as long as the righteous experience bliss.

If there should still be any doubt in anyone's mind whether the occupants of hell suffer eternal conscious misery, we can settle the matter by an appeal to two passages from the book of Revelation. Those who worship the beast and have received his mark are described as drinking the wine of the wrath of God which is mixed in full strength, and such will be

> tormented with fire and brimstone in the presence of the holy angels and in the presence of the Lamb. And the smoke of their torment goes up forever and ever; and they have no rest day and night, those who worship the

beast and his image, and whoever receives the mark of his name. (Revelation 14:10-11)

Notice that the fire does not annihilate the wicked but torments them. There, in the presence of the holy angels and the Lamb, there will be no periods of rest during which the wicked are unconscious of torment. They will never slip into peaceful nonexistence.

In Revelation 20 we have a similar scene. The beast and the false prophet have been thrown into the lake of fire, and Satan has been released to deceive the nations for one thousand years. At the end of that period, Satan is cast into the lake of fire. Notice carefully that *the beast and the false prophet have not been annihilated during those one thousand years in hell.* The fire has not consumed them: "And the devil who deceived them was thrown into the lake of fire and brimstone, where the beast and the false prophet are also; and they will be tormented day and night forever and ever" (20:10).

Hence, the teachings of universalism and annihilationism come to their deceptive end. Eternal, conscious torment is clearly taught—*there is no other honest interpretation of these passages.*

When we say that God should save everyone (as the universalists say) or that He is obligated to obliterate the wicked (as the annihilationists say), we make salvation a matter of justice. But the Bible teaches plainly that salvation is a matter of mercy, not justice. Thus if God wishes to bestow mercy on some and display His justice in the lives of others, He has that right.

HELL AND THE JUSTICE OF GOD

Read the literature of the universalists or annihilationists and you cannot help but suspect that their theories are believed not so much because the Bible supports them but because of the difficulty of harmonizing eternal punishment with the justice and love of God. Pinnock, you will recall, lamented that it was difficult enough to explain evil to the unbelieving world without having to explain hell, too. Sensitive Christians, he says, cannot believe in eternal, conscious punishment.

To us as humans, everlasting punishment is disproportionate to the offense committed. God appears cruel, unjust, sadistic, and vindictive. The purpose of punishment, we are told, is always redemptive. Rehabilitation is the goal of all prison sentences. The concept of a place where there will be endless punishment without any possibility of parole or reform seems unjust.

As far as we know, if He had so desired, God could have created a universe free from sin and the corruption of rebellion. If Adam and Eve had had natures that abhorred sin and loved obedience they could have made a voluntary choice to follow God's orders. Lucifer could have been either exterminated or confined to another planet. Even better, Lucifer himself could have been created with a nature that would have never desired to oppose God. Those are just some of the possibilities.

Yet the fact is that God set up a world in which there would be rebellion and the awful consequences of sin, a universe with both a heaven and a hell. Since we know that the Almighty works all things according to the council of His own will, we must believe that even the unbelievers in hell will bring honor to His name and magnify His attributes, among them His attribute of justice.

How can hell be just? The following observations may not answer all of our questions, but hopefully they will help us begin to see hell from God's perspective.

Men and women will be judged on the basis of knowledge. Christ taught, "And that slave who knew his master's will and did not get ready or act in accord with his will, shall receive many lashes, but the one who did not know it, and committed deeds worthy of a flogging, will receive but few. And from everyone who has been given much shall much be required; and to whom they entrusted much, of him they will ask all the more" (Luke 12:47-48).

Those who live without specific knowledge about Christ will be judged by the light of nature and their own conscience (Romans 1:20; 2:14-16). That does not mean that those who respond to general revelation will be automatically saved, for no one lives up to all that he knows. That is why a personal knowledge of Christ is needed for salvation. "And there is salvation in no one else; for there is no other name under heaven that has been given among men, by which we must be saved" (Acts 4:12).

But the light of God in nature and in the human conscience is still a sufficient basis for judgment. Whatever the degree of punishment, it will fit the offense exactly, for God is meticulously just. Those who believe in

Christ experience mercy; those who do not (either because they have never heard of Him or they reject what they know of Him) will receive justice. Either way, God is glorified.

Man's responsibility is therefore based on knowledge and performance. That is why at the Great White Throne judgment where all unbelievers appear, the books are opened and the dead are judged "according to their deeds" (Revelation 20:13). Once again I emphasize that their deeds cannot save them, for by the works of the law no flesh can be justified in His sight. Yet their performance does determine their punishment.

Think of how accurately God will judge every unbeliever! Each day of every life will be analyzed in minute detail. The hidden thoughts and motives of each hour will be replayed, along with all actions and attitudes. The words spoken in secret will be made public, the intentions of the heart displayed for all to see. They will have no attorney to whom they may appeal, no loopholes by which they can escape. Nothing but bare, indisputable facts.

I believe that the balance of justice will be so accurate that a pornographer will wish he had never published such material; a thief will wish he had earned an honest living; and an adulterer will regret that he lived an immoral life. Faithfulness to his marriage vows would not have earned him a place in heaven to be sure, but it would have made his existence in hell slightly more bearable.

Before God, no motives will be misinterpreted, no extenuating circumstances thrown out of court. The woman who seduced the man will receive her fair share of punishment, and the man who allowed himself to be seduced will receive his. All blame will be accurately proportioned.

We all agree that heaven is a comforting doctrine. What is often overlooked is that hell is comforting, too. Our newspapers are filled with stories of rape, child abuse, and a myriad of injustices. Every court case ever tried on earth will be re-opened; every action and motive will be meticulously inspected and just retribution meted out. In the presence of an all-knowing God there will be no unsolved murders, no unknown child abductor, and no hidden bribe.

UNBELIEVERS ARE ETERNALLY GUILTY

Hell exists because unbelievers are eternally guilty. The powerful lesson to be learned is that no human being's suffering can ever be a payment for sin. If our suffering could erase even the most insignificant sin, then those in hell would eventually

25

be freed after their debt was paid. But all human goodness and suffering from the beginning of time, if added together, could not cancel so much as a single sin.

> Could my tears forever flow,
> Could my zeal no respite know,
> All for sin could not atone;
> Thou must save and Thou alone.
> ("Rock of Ages")

Sir Francis Newport, who ridiculed Christianity, is quoted as saying these terrifying words on his deathbed:

> Oh that I was to lie a thousand years upon the fire that never is quenched, to purchase the favor of God, and be united to him again! But it is a fruitless wish. Millions and millions of years would bring me no nearer to the end of my torments than one poor hour. Oh, eternity, eternity! forever and forever! Oh, the insufferable pains of hell![5]

He was quite right in saying that a million years in hell could not purchase salvation. Tragically, he did not cast himself upon the mercy of God in Christ. Since no man's works or sufferings can save him, he must bear the full weight of his sin throughout eternity.

We must confess that we do not know exactly how much punishment is enough for those who have sinned against God. We may think we know what God is like, but we see through a glass darkly. The famous theologian Jonathan Edwards said that the reason we find hell so offensive is because of our insensitivity to sin.

What if, from God's viewpoint, the greatness of sin is determined by the greatness of the One against whom it is committed? Then the guilt of sin is infinite because it is a violation of the character of an infinite Being. What if, in the nature of God, it is deemed that such infinite sins deserve an infinite penalty, a penalty which no one can ever repay?

We must realize that God did not choose the attributes He possesses. Because He has existed from all eternity His attributes were already determined from eternity past. If God had not possessed love and mercy throughout all eternity, we might have been created by a malicious and cruel being who delighted in watching His creatures suffer perpetual torment. Fortunately, that is not the case. The Bible tells of the love and mercy of God; He does not delight in the death of the wicked. But it also has much to say about His justice and the fact that even the wicked in hell will glorify Him. To put it clearly, we must accept God as He is revealed in the Bible whether He suits our preferences or not.

When Paul was defending the doctrine of God's sovereignty in choosing a remnant of the Jewish nation for special favors, he knew that it would elicit loud objections from his readers. But he was undeterred by their protests and asserted that the clay did not have the right to question the potter. If God wanted to make His wrath and power known, He had the right to "[endure] with much patience vessels of wrath prepared for destruction" (Romans 9:22).

It is absurd in the extreme to say, "I don't want to be in heaven with a God who sends people to hell. . . . I would rather go to hell and defy Him." I can't exaggerate the foolishness of those who think they can oppose God to their own satisfaction or to His detriment! In Psalm 2 we read that God sits in the heavens and laughs at those who think they can defy Him. Like the mouse who thinks it can stand against the farmer's plow or the rowboat poised to thwart the path of an aircraft carrier, it is insanity for man to think that he can oppose the living God who is angry with sinners and is bent on taking vengeance on those who oppose Him.

Even as we look at the suffering in the world today, we should not be surprised that God allows multitudes to live in eternal misery. Think of the vast amount of suffering (preventable suffering, if you please) that God has allowed on this earth. An earthquake in Mexico kills twenty thousand, a tidal wave in Bangladesh kills fifty thousand, and famines in the world cause twenty thousand deaths every single day! Who can begin to calculate the amount of emotional pain experienced by babies, children, and adults? Yet we know that strengthening the earth's crust, sending rain, and withholding floods could all be accomplished by a word from the Almighty.

If God has allowed people to live in untold misery for thousands of years, why would it be inconsistent for Him to allow misery to continue forever? Charles Hodge asks, "If the highest glory of God and the good of the universe have been promoted by the past sinfulness and misery of men, why may not those objects be promoted by what is declared to be future?"[6]

If our concept of justice differs from God's, we can be quite sure that He will be unimpressed by our attempts to get Him to see things from our point of view. No one is God's counselor; no one instructs or corrects Him. He does not look to us for input on how to run His universe.

We now return to a study of the doctrine of hell, noting the Greek words used to describe it in the New Testament. Then we will glimpse its torments in a story told by Christ Himself.

GREEK WORDS FOR HELL

The New Testament uses three different Greek words for *hell*. One is *tartarus*, used in 2 Peter 2:4 for the abode of evil angels who sinned during the time of Noah. "For . . . God did not spare angels when they sinned, but cast them into hell and committed them to pits of darkness, reserved for judgment." In Jude 6 the word *tartarus* is used similarly.

The second and most often used word for hell in the New Testament is *gehenna*, a word for hell already used by the Jews before the time of Christ. The word is derived from the Hebrew "valley of Hinnom" found in the Old Testament (Joshua 15:8; 2 Kings 23:10; Nehemiah 11:30). In that valley outside Jerusalem the Jews gave human sacrifices to pagan deities. There, too, the garbage of the city was thrown, where it bred worms. That explains why Christ referred to hell as the place where "their worm does not die, and the fire is not quenched" (Mark 9:44, 46, 48).

This picture of an unclean dump where fires and worms never die became to the Jewish mind an appropriate description of the ultimate fate of all idolaters. Thus the word became applied to the ultimate *gehenna*. The Jews taught, and Christ confirmed, that the wicked would suffer there forever. Body and soul would be in eternal torment.

For years liberal scholars taught (and some sentimentalists still do) that Christ, who stressed the love of God, could never be party to the doctrine of hell. Yet significantly, of the twelve times the word *gehenna* is used in the New Testament, eleven times it came from the mouth of our Lord. Indeed, He spoke more about hell than about heaven.

The third word is *Hades*, which is not a reference to hell but rather to the place where unbelievers presently go to await the Great White Throne judgment. The word, however, is translated "hell" in the King James version of the Bible. Most other translations simply leave it untranslated as *Hades* so that it might be properly distinguished from hell.

Purgatory has no basis in the New Testament but is an idea borrowed from mythologies about the existence of a place of temporary punishment from which one would finally be extricated. The reason it was incorporated into the teaching of the church during the Dark Ages is because it corresponded so directly with the defective view of justification that was prevalent at that time. Indeed, it is not too strong to say that the medieval understanding of justification necessitated purgatory.

Specifically, the belief was that God makes people righteous through their participation in the sacraments and their good works. But the people had no assurance that they had ever accumulated enough righteousness to gain God's approval. Purgatory was thus the place for temporal punishment of sins; they would be "purged" from sins so that they would become righteous enough to enter heaven. Later the notion arose that it was possible to pay a fee to the church for relatives so that their time in purgatory would be shortened.

Those abuses angered Luther, and his efforts at reformation were begun with the intention of basing theology on the Bible rather than on tradition and pagan mythologies. The New Testament doctrine of justification will be explained at the end of this booklet.

What will the suffering of hell be like? We must guard against undue speculation since the Scriptures do not describe the torments of hell in specifics. We must not fall into the error of the medievals who described hell with the vivid details of a guide taking tourists through the Vatican. Yet, Jesus told a story that does give us a glimpse of hell, or more accurately, a glimpse of Hades, which is a prelude to the final place of eternal punishment.

CHARACTERISTICS OF HELL

Often when Christ confronted the self-righteous Pharisees, He used a parable or a true story to awaken them to God's priorities over and against their own. On this occasion the topic was their love of money and disregard for the spiritual values of love and truth. To illustrate the fact that "that which is highly esteemed among men is detestable in the sight of God"(Luke 16:15), Christ told a story (it is not called a parable) of a rich man who ended up in Hades in contrast to a poor man who was carried away by angels into Abraham's bosom (heaven). Christ's point was to show how the fortunes of the two men were reversed in the afterlife. The rich man was in torment; the poor man was in bliss.

And in Hades he lifted up his eyes, being in torment, and saw Abraham far away, and Lazarus in his bosom. And he cried out and said, "Father Abraham, have mercy on me, and send Lazarus, that he may dip the tip of his finger in water and cool off my tongue; for I am in agony in this flame."

But Abraham said, "Child, remember that during your life you received your good things, and likewise Lazarus bad things; but now he is being comforted here, and you are in agony. And besides all this, between us and you there is a great chasm fixed, in order that those who wish to come over from here to you may not be able, and that none may cross over from there to us."

And he said, "Then I beg you, Father, that you send him to my father's house—for I have five brothers—that he may warn them, lest they also come to this place of torment."

But Abraham said, "They have Moses and the Prophets; let them hear them."

But he said, "No, Father Abraham, but if someone goes to them from the dead, they will repent!"

But he said to him, "If they do not listen to Moses and the Prophets, neither will they be persuaded if someone rises from the dead." (Luke 16:23-31)

What can we say about the rich man's experience in Hades? Let me remind you once again that he was not yet—indeed he *is* not yet—in hell. Though hell will be far worse than Hades, this story does give a telling glimpse of what the fate of unbelievers will be.

A PLACE OF TORMENT

Usually when we think of hell, we think of fire since Christ spoke of the "fire of hell." In Revelation we read of "the lake of fire and brimstone."

There is no reason the torments of hell could not include physical fire, since the bodies of those present will have been re-created and made indestructible. Unlike our present bodies, those of the resurrected dead will not burn up or be extinguished. Literal fire is a possibility.

However, there is another kind of fire that will be in hell, a fire that may be worse than literal fire. That is the fire of unfulfilled passion, the fire of desires that are never satisfied. Perpetually burning lusts never subside, and the tortured conscience burns but is never sedated or appeased. There will be increased desire with decreased satisfaction.

In Hades the rich man experiences a preview of the torments of hell. Notice that in the story his physical desires were still active; he was thirsty, wishing for a drop of water to cool his tongue. Let us remember that the people in hell will be the same people they were on earth, with the same desires, aspirations, and feelings. Yet their needs will not be met.

In Proverbs we read of the insatiable desires of the netherworld and a man's lusts. "Sheol and Abaddon are never satisfied, nor are the eyes of man ever satisfied" (27:20). An alcoholic will thirst for a drop of liquor in hell but will not get it; a drug addict will crave a shot of heroin; the immoral man will burn with sexual desire but will never be gratified. The body will be aflame with lusts, but the fire will never be quenched. It's as if God is saying, "On earth you did not let Me satisfy you but turned to your own lusts; now you will find that those lusts can only drive you to despair."

Hell, then, is the raw soul joined to an indestructible body, exposed to its own sin for eternity. Hell is the place of unquenchable, raging, unmet emotional needs, without painkillers or sedation.

The rich man was permitted to speak to Abraham, but there could be no direct, intimate communication with those in heaven. His request for a drop of water to cool his tongue was denied because he was getting his just desserts, and furthermore, between them was an unbridgeable chasm.

Does that mean that there will be some form of communication between those in heaven and the occupants of hell? Not necessarily. There is evidence in the New Testament that "Abraham's bosom" was transferred directly into the presence of Christ at the ascension. Even more important, however, the Scriptures teach that Hades shall be thrown into hell, the lake of fire, after the final judgment. "And the sea gave up the dead which were in it, and death and Hades gave up the dead which were in them; and they were judged, every one of them according to their deeds" (Revelation 20:13).

However, those who are in hell will be tormented in the presence of Christ and the holy angels (Revelation 14:10). It is generally believed that the righteous shall behold the terrors of hell, and part of the suffering of the unbelievers will be to see a friend or relative in eternal bliss. Though that is not expressly stated,

God often invites righteous people or angels to behold the judgment He inflicts upon the wicked (Psalm 46:8-9; Isaiah 66:23-24; Revelation 19:17-21). Famous British preacher Charles Haddon Spurgeon wrote, "If there be one thing in hell worse than another, it will be seeing the saints in heaven. . . . Husband, there is your wife in heaven and you are among the damned. And do you see your father? Your child is before the throne, and you accursed of God and man are in hell!"

If believers do witness these events, we can be sure that they will agree completely with the justice displayed by God, for then they shall see all things from His point of view. Thus, the righteous can enjoy the bliss of heaven knowing full well the fate of the wicked in hell.

Will there be communication among those who occupy hell? We cannot say, for the Scriptures are silent. C. S. Lewis believed there would not be, stating that hell is a place of solitude. Jonathan Edwards believed that if unbelievers are next to one another they will only add to each other's agony through expressions of hatred, accusations, and curses. Of one thing we can be absolutely certain: no comfort will be derived from the presence of others. Consumed with the torment of raging, unforgiven sin, those in hell will never find comfort again.

Though Dante added many of his own ideas to the superstitions of his day when he wrote *The Inferno*, the sign he read in the vestibule of hell does portray the biblical teaching of hopelessness and abandonment.

> I am the way to the city of woe.
> I am the way to a forsaken people.
> I am the way into eternal sorrow.
>
> Sacred justice moved my architect.
> I was raised here by divine omnipotence,
> Primordial love and ultimate intellect.
>
> Only those elements time cannot wear
> Were made before me, and beyond time I stand.
> Abandon all hope ye who enter here.

Jonathan Edwards pointed out that those in hell will have no reason for entertaining any secret hope that after being in the flames many ages God will take pity on them and release them. God, says Edwards, will not be any more inclined to release them after a million ages than He was at the very first moment. Little wonder, Edwards said, that any description we give of hell can be but a faint representation of the reality!

A PLACE OF AN ACTIVE CONSCIENCE AND A GOOD MEMORY

The rich man asked Abraham to let Lazarus return to his (the rich man's) house to warn his five brothers that they might not come to the same place of torment. There in Hades he expressed concern for those whom he loved; he remembered who he was and what happened on earth. The similarity between who he had been on earth and who he was now in Hades should not escape us.

Incredibly, this man became interested in missions! He would like Lazarus to return from the dead to dramatize to his brothers the need to prepare for the life to come. This man who lived in luxury on earth and saw no special need for God now suddenly saw that one's relationship with God is of highest priority. Apparently he knew more about the way to God then we might have expected. He specifically asked Abraham to return and preach *repentance* to his brothers.

Abraham's answer is instructive: "They have Moses and the Prophets; let them hear them."

The rich man replied, "No, Father Abraham, but if someone goes to them from the dead, they will repent!"

Abraham replied, "If they do not listen to Moses and the Prophets, neither will they be persuaded if someone rises from the dead."

How true! When Christ told this story, He had not yet been put to death and resurrected. But today, even after His resurrection, many men and women do not believe. Yet Christ taught that His own resurrection was the only sign He would give to the world. "A man convinced against his will is of the same opinion still."

Far from thinking that the presence of his brothers would give him some much needed company in Hades, this man was more than willing not to see them again if only they would be in a place of comfort rather than torment! Those in hell will be the same people they were on earth with the same memories, identity, and feelings.

A PLACE OF ETERNITY

We have already established the fact that the Bible teaches that hell is

41

unending. But now we must pause to try to understand what that means. How long is eternity?

Visualize a bird coming to earth every million years and taking one grain of sand with it to a distant planet. At that rate it would take thousands of billions of years before the bird had carried away a single handful of sand. Now let's expand that illustration and think how long it would take the bird to move the Oak Street Beach in Chicago and then the other thousands of beaches around the world. After that the bird could begin on the mountains and the earth's crust.

By the time the bird transported the entire earth to the far-off planet, eternity would not have officially begun. Strictly speaking one cannot begin an infinite series, for a beginning implies an end. In other words, we might say that after the bird has done his work, those in eternity will not be one step closer to having their suffering alleviated. There is no such thing as half an eternity.

The most sobering thought that could ever cross our minds is the fact that the rich man in Hades referred to above has not *yet* received the drop of water for which he so desperately longed. Today, as you read this booklet, he is still there awaiting the final judgment of the lake of fire. Eternity endures, and it endures *forever.*

A PLACE OF EASY ACCESS BUT NO EXIT

We could wish that the signs along the pathway to hell were clearly marked. "Turn Left for Eternal Destruction" or "Follow These Truths to Everlasting Blessedness"—such signs, if accurate, would be of help in our journey through life. Regrettably, the way is a bit more difficult.

Christ in effect taught that *the path to hell is labeled as the path to heaven.* There are two roads, He said: a wide one that leads to everlasting destruction and a narrow one that leads to eternal life. Many who are on the broad way are actually confident that they will arrive at the right destination. A recent poll showed that about three out of four Americans believe that their chances of getting to heaven are good or excellent.

Jonathan Edwards, whom we have already quoted, gave more consideration to the doctrine of hell than any other theologian. His sermon "Sinners in the Hands of an Angry God" kept audiences spellbound, stripping from them any objections or excuses they might have had against the doctrine of hell. He made the point that there are some people

43

now living for whom God has more anger than some who are in Hades (he called it hell) who have already died. Therefore it was only the mercy of God that kept them from plunging into the abyss:

> There is nothing that keeps wicked men at any one moment out of hell, but the mere pleasure of God. . . . There is no want in God's power to cast wicked men into hell at any moment. . . . They deserve to be cast into hell, so divine justice never stands in the way. . . . They are now the objects of that very same anger and wrath that is expressed in the torments of hell . . . yea God is a great deal more angry with great numbers that are now on the earth, yea doubtless with some who reread this book, who it may be are at ease, than he is with many of those who are now in the flames of hell.
>
> Unconverted men walk over the pit of hell on a rotten covering, and there are innumerable places in this covering so weak that they will not bear their weight, and these places are not seen. . . . There is the dreadful pit of the glowing flames of the wrath of God; there is hell's wide gaping mouth open; and you have nothing to stand upon, nor anything to take hold of, there is

nothing between you and hell but air; it is only the power and mere pleasure of God that holds you up. . . . His wrath burns against you like fire; he looks upon you as worthy of nothing else than to be thrown into the fire. . . . you hang by the slender thread, with the flames of divine wrath flashing about it and ready every moment to singe it, and burn it asunder.[7]

Edwards concluded his sermon with an appeal to men to take advantage of the mercy of God in Christ. Just think, he said, of what those who are in hell would give for one single hour of opportunity to respond to God's saving grace!

Just as there have been believers who have already seen glimpses of heaven before they died, so some unbelievers have already described the torments of Hades as they slipped from this world into the next. The skeptic Robert Ingersoll said, "You do not have to tell me there is no hell, for I already feel its flames." Others have confessed to seeing demons waiting to escort them into that fearful abyss.

Let me ask, Which path are you on? Who is qualified to tell us which signposts are accurate and which ones are erected by deceivers who snare the wary into a false hope? Obviously you and I are not in a position to resolve such issues since they fall outside the scope of human knowledge. What we need is someone who has the authority to speak for God, someone who is not limited to human inclinations and observations.

The one man—the only man—with such impressive credentials is Christ. He came down from heaven as the second member of the Trinity to reveal God the Father and to give His life as a sacrifice for sins. He spoke about the hereafter with confidence—referring to hell more often than to heaven.

First of all we must see that Christ alone is the way to God the Father: "I am the way, and the truth, and the life; no one comes to the Father, but through Me" (John 14:6).

Second, we must understand that Christ is the only one who is qualified to lead us to God because His death was a sacrifice for sinners. He satisfied God's just requirements so that sinners could be declared righteous—so righteous that they can go to heaven immediately at death without the need for purgatory.

Christ bore our hell so that we would not have to bear it ourselves. Sin demands an infinite payment; only Christ who is Himself God could make such a payment.

How do we receive these benefits? We must acknowledge our sinfulness and helplessness, confessing our inability to save ourselves. Then we must willfully transfer all of our trust to Christ alone for our acceptance before God. "But as many as received Him, to them He gave the right to become children of God, even to those who believe in His name" (John 1:12).

Let me warn you not to trust in your baptism, the sacraments, or any other ritual. Only those who are born again of the Holy Spirit will enter the kingdom of heaven (John 3:5).

Many years ago a father and his daughter were walking through the grass on the Canadian prairie. In the distance they saw a prairie fire which eventually, they realized, would engulf them. The father knew that there was only one way of escape: they would build a fire right where they were and burn a large area of grass. When the huge fire drew near, the child was terrified, but the father assured her that they would not be burned because *they were standing where the fire had already been.*

The fire of God's wrath fell on Christ so that we might be shielded from His wrath. Faith placed personally and exclusively in Christ can exempt us from punishment. Only those who flee to Him will escape the flames.

It is a fearful thing to fall into the hands of the living God unprepared.

Notes

1. "Universalism—Is It Heretical?" *Scottish Journal of Theology*, June 1949, p. 155.
2. Percy Dearmer, *The Legend of Hell* (London: Cassell, 1929), pp. 74-75.
3. Edward Fudge, *The Fire That Consumes* (Houston, Texas: Providential, 1982), pp. 48-49.
4. Robert Morey, *Death and the Afterlife* (Minneapolis: Bethany, 1984), p. 90.
5. Walter B. Knight, *Knight's Master Book of New Illustrations* (Grand Rapids: Eerdman's, 1956), p. 159.
6. Charles Hodge, *Systematic Theology*, vol. 3, pt. 4 (Grand Rapids: Eerdman's, reprint, 1982), p. 879.
7. Warren Wiersbe, *Treasury of the World's Great Sermons* (Grand Rapids: Kregel, 1977), pp. 198-205.

Moody Press, a ministry of the Moody Bible Institute, is designed for education, evangelization, and edification. If we may assist you in knowing more about Christ and the Christian life, please write us without obligation: Moody Press, c/o MLM, Chicago, Illinois 60610.